STAY THE COURSE

Adam Packard

EAGLE ONE
PUBLISHING

ISBN: 978-0-9842703-2-3

Printed in the United States of America

Eagle One Publishing
PO Box 26173
Salt Lake City, UT 84126
www.eagleonepublishing.com

THANK YOU...

To my brother Jeff, who initially led the charge and got our family started in building SendOutCards as a business, and for being a great role model. To my father, Jim, who started me on a journey of personal development at a young age, and for being an incredible mentor in all that I do. And for my mother, Sherry, the ultimate giver, always encouraging, supporting, and inspiring me—thanks for telling me I'm a good writer. This book is a result of you telling me that over and over again!

Stay the Course

Lessons Learned on My SendOutCards Journey

PRAISE FOR
STAY THE COURSE

"I loved this book. The reason why is because it is not a book about how to do the business. The *how* is very easy: call my people, walk them through sending a card. Adam dug deeper and wanted to understand why people are doing this business. When you figure out what you want and why you want it, you can achieve anything! I highly recommend this book to all team members and people who want to succeed."

JEFF PACKARD

"I have known Adam from the time he was a baby in this industry. He has never been afraid of learning what it takes to be successful. He is teachable, and that is what makes Adam such a phenomenal leader.

Adam has put together a great compilation of what to do and what not to do when it comes to building a successful SendOutCards business. He hasn't held anything back. This book is a must for every new, used, and old distributor—especially those who want to crack the code."

DEMARR ZIMMERMAN

"Adam's insight into what it takes to be successful in network marketing is right on target. He is wise beyond his years. As his dad, I can tell you that he has always been a leader, whether it was wanting the ball in his hands in the championship baseball game or taking the final shot in basketball. It's not surprising that he has built one of the largest organizations in SendOutCards by utilizing his leadership abilities. I constantly learn from Adam, and now everyone else can too."

JIM PACKARD

"Maybe you are new to SendOutCards, or maybe you have been in for a year or years. It doesn't matter—all of the tips, strategies and advice in this book are timeless and we all need to consistently implement them. I recently was preparing for a Super Saturday with Adam. I was trying to go back over the key points Adam has driven home in one-on-one calls and conference calls to lead me from a stay-at-home mom to Executive with over 1,000 distributors in 3.5 years. I consider this book a survival guide that I recommend everyone read and hand down to their teams."

AMY KOLLN

FOREWORD

Around the time Adam asked me to put together the introduction to this book, I was visiting the SendOutCards company headquarters in Salt Lake City. The next morning, SendOutCards founder Kody Bateman was driving me to the airport to catch a 7 a.m. flight to Phoenix (unusual for me— usually I'm not up that early in the morning!).

It was still dark and cold in the early morning hours, and we both noticed something interesting: There were lots and lots of cars on the highway. I thought, *Most of the people are tired and a little frustrated that they must continue to set an alarm clock each day and get up before the sun rises to report to a job that they really don't like that much. Many have become numb to the pain that they feel leaving their families each day to report to a boss they can barely tolerate.* I looked at their faces. They didn't look too happy. Really, they looked quite miserable. It's the price people pay to get a paycheck.

At least one hour every day is spent on the commute. Five hours per week, 20 hours per month, 240 hours per year. The price we will pay for a paycheck. Those same hours invested in a SendOutCards business can set you free. Can an hour a day really set you free? It all depends on what you do with that hour.

Adam's book will help you know what to do.

What would your life be like if you could throw away the alarm clock? Imagine waking up each morning when your body wants to wake up! Imagine spending quality time with your family each day without being rushed to work for a business you really don't like.

For 17 years I set an alarm clock each morning. I can remember it quite clearly: each morning violently yanking me out of a deep, peaceful sleep. Beep...beep...beep...BEEP! I used to hate that! Your life doesn't have to be that way. It's not natural. It ages you! And there are options.

Imagine a blank sheet of paper with a horizontal line drawn across the bottom of the page. Below that line is 90 percent of the adult population. Ninety percent live in quiet desperation. They are being held captive by the choices they have made. Most make less than $50,000 per year and are one emergency away from going broke. Below this line lies struggle, uncertainty, and fear.

Now imagine a line drawn horizontally across the top. Above this line lies 3 percent of the population. Three percent are financially free. They have residual income and true security. Most are self-made, but it's actually easier to live above the line than below it. Most do what they do because they love it, and they don't have to go to work for money any longer.

What they know and what they do are quite simple. But to the 90 percent that live below the bottom line, it's a big mystery.

Imagine a ladder taking you from below that bottom line to the 3 percent up top. There are four things that will lift you up from struggle to freedom:

- A personal development plan
- A system for nurturing relationships in your life and creating new and dynamic ones
- An income opportunity
- A network of success-minded people

These things constitute the process for going from below the line to above the line. These things can set you free and bring more joy and fulfillment to your life.

Yes, there is a price to pay to build a successful network-marketing business; you'll learn it all in this book. But the rewards for paying the price are like no other. You are going to pay a price. The question is, *Is the price you are paying worth your life?*

Adam asked me why I do SendOutCards. My answer is simple:

1) To have fun. Sending cards and receiving cards is fun. Receiving residual checks in the mail is fun. Hanging out with great people is fun.

2) To be free. Residual income allows you to live the life that *you* want to live. You get to travel the world, hang out with your family and close friends, and buy gifts for those you care about. When you spend your money, it comes back again next month whether you go to work or not!

3) To do good in the world. You have the opportunity to change peoples' lives by offering them a way to appreciate others and make a great income. There is nothing like it!

And when I ask people if they want these three things, they light up. Everyone wants to *have fun, be free, and do good in the world*.

By the way, you can start doing these three things right away, and you don't need SendOutCards to get started. If you are looking to create a better life, adopt these three things right away; the money will follow. I think you'll see that those who *live* these three things create the income at a record rate. You get to have fun right now. You get to be free right now, and you get to do good in the world right now.

So get ready for the ride of your life. It's all here in this book.

JORDAN ADLER

SendOutCards No. 1 team builder and money earner

Author of *Beach Money: Creating your*

Dream Life through Network Marketing

INTRODUCTION

I was in Atlanta at the SendOutCards Friday night leadership event before our Treat 'em Right Seminar. I was asked to speak for 15 minutes on the topic of my choice. I had thought about that speaking assignment for the past few weeks, and after seeing David Frey, Senior Executive and one of our top team builders, do a PowerPoint at the New Orleans executive retreat, I thought, "I should do that too!"

I started preparing a series of slides titled "Stay the Course." I thought of the lessons I had learned in SendOutCards and how it would be helpful to share those lessons with others in this business. I had fun making the presentation, and ideas and thoughts kept coming to me.

What was supposed to be a 15-minute presentation ended up lasting closer to 40 minutes. Afterwards, Jordan Adler, the first to reach the top rank of Eagle in SendOutCards, came to me and said, "Adam, everyone in SendOutCards needs to hear that. You just condensed five years worth of training calls into a PowerPoint." I thought, *Nice compliment!* So for those who are wanting to learn from my successes and mistakes, this is for you.

WHAT THIS BOOK IS

This is simply a compilation of lessons I have learned and things that have helped me in my SendOutCards journey. I have been privileged to be part of a great team, with my brother Jeff, my father Jim, and my close friend Jordan Adler.

I have spent lots of time with the top leaders and heard their challenges, their frustrations, and what keeps them going. By no means do I have all the answers; this business is always a learning process, whether you have 100 reps or 50,000 reps.

WHAT THIS BOOK IS NOT

This is not a "how-to" guide. It was never my intention to tell someone how to run their business. The beautiful part about network marketing is that you can run your business any way you want. As long as you stay in compliance with the company and follow some basic rules, you can work this business a number of different ways. I am not telling you my way is the right way, so if you disagree with what I say, that's totally fine. My goal is to share the mistakes I made (and that you can avoid) and the steps leading to my success that you can implement too.

WHY I WROTE IT

I see a lot of distributors get into SendOutCards and struggle. They start with high expectations, but they don't realize what it will take to build a successful business. People are always asking me, "What do you do? How did you build your business? What lessons did you learn? What would you change if you could start over?" I love to write and thought the best way to spread my answers was to get the details down on paper to share with anyone who wanted to take a look. Some of the things I've learned kept me going when I was frustrated, when I was having a bad day, when things were not going the way I wanted—or not growing as quickly as I wanted. If I can help just one person keep moving forward, this book is a success. I want to see everyone involved in SendOutCards reach whatever level of success they desire. If you know what it takes to build the business, you will be more likely to keep going when you hit roadblocks and face challenges.

WHO I AM

I started working SendOutCards in August of 2005. Initially I did not want to build this as a business. Thanks to my brother getting a fast start and showing me how he was making money, I dove in head first and haven't looked back. I have zero previous experience in network marketing. I didn't have a network of people to call. I was 26, and saw the dream that network marketing could provide, and I went for it. I built a team of a few thousand that continues to grow, and I have created a residual income for myself that has allowed me to take control of my life.

Am I content? No. Am I happy? Yes. I will always be building SendOutCards because I love the crusade and I love the challenge. I love helping my team members quit their jobs, take their dream vacations, stay home with their kids, and realize their goals. I want to have some part of helping a lot of people get to the point where they have more choices. Life is too short to not do what you want to do when you want to do it.

WHO THIS BOOK IS FOR

Whether you are brand new to SendOutCards and looking to do big things or have been involved for awhile and need a kick in the pants, this is for you. This is written for those who want the big checks, who are ready to take charge of their lives and their SendOutCards business—because it *can* happen for you.

We all learn from each other. I have learned great things from the leaders in this company. If you knew why others gave up and quit, wouldn't that be helpful? If you knew what helped others succeed, wouldn't that be helpful? This should be your goal—know what works, know how to avoid the things that caused others to quit, and apply the lessons to your business. I look forward to seeing you walk across the stage to accept your promotion in SendOutCards. We all deserve the best.

CHAPTER 1

Treat it as a Business

If you don't have a plan, you are probably a part of

someone else's plan, and they probably don't have much

planned for you!

JIM ROHN

The beautiful thing about SendOutCards is you can start your own business for a few hundred dollars. The challenge about SendOutCards is that you can start your business for a few hundred dollars. This is a business that can pay you thousands, if not millions, of dollars over the course of your lifetime. Because the investment is only a few hundred dollars, many people do not treat this like a business that can pay you that way. What do you risk losing if you don't do anything to grow your business? Just a few hundred bucks.

I know you want to make the most of your business or you wouldn't be reading this. You want the business that allows you freedom in every possible way. Can you imagine what would happen if the owner of a Subway franchise, who spent hundreds of thousands of dollars to get started, didn't treat his or her business like a business? Not only do you need to treat your business as the million-dollar business it is, but you need to have a system in place that you follow—a system that has been proven to work. The reason McDonald's grows? They have a system so simple that high school kids can run it. We have a system in SendOutCards as well. I'm not going to get into the system behind our business, as I'm hoping your sponsor has plugged you into some basic training, but follow it because it works! It's all spelled out at www.thedaily8.com.

KEEP SCORE

One of the main components of the SendOutCards business-building system is the use of The Daily 8 program and the Scorecard. Whether you print the forms and keep track or use The Daily 8 planner (which I recommend), you need to *keep score*! What can't be measured can't be managed!

Back when I first started working SendOutCards, we didn't have The Daily 8 or the Scorecard. However, I still kept track of my activities *daily*. At that time I kept track of cards and DVDs sent, gift account walkthroughs done, new contacts added, and new signups. I used a dry erase board on my wall to keep track of activities, and I knew if I completed those activities, my business would grow. Trust me, if you keep score and see zeroes for your activities, you have no one to blame but yourself!

ACCOUNTABILITY

This step is *huge*. You need to find an accountability partner. It can be your upline, your business partner, your spouse, your friend, someone you meet in SendOutCards that is not part of your team, or just someone with similar SendOutCards goals. My accountability partner since I started this business has been my older brother Jeff. At first it was more competition than accountability, but it worked. I knew if I heard him up and making calls, I needed to be doing the same thing. He saw my numbers and always wanted to keep up, and vice versa. We pushed each other. We have now become less competitive, but we still hold each other accountable for what we do. I have some team members who text me their numbers daily, and believe me, when you text zeros to your upline, it doesn't take much for the message to sink in. Zeros mean your business will not grow. Find someone you can be accountable to and don't fudge your numbers! Be truthful and honest, and everyday activities will lead to your success.

FOCUS ON ACTIONS

When building my SendOutCards business, I focused on how many people I was bringing in. While that is obviously important, you can't always control who enters your business and when they come in. All you can control is your actions. That is why The Daily 8 and keeping score is so important. If you are doing these activities, the results you want will follow.

One key to success for my father, who enrolls about 70 percent of the people he introduces to SendOutCards, is his goal to simply show them the program and the business. He doesn't convince them to join. He takes the focus off "trying to sign them up" and lets them enjoy the process. You can control how many cards you send, how many DVDs you hand out, how many magazines you have in play, how many walk-throughs you do, and how many guests you invite to events and conference calls. You can't control when someone joins, so don't stress about it—only focus on what you can control.

CHAPTER 2

Your Foundation

This business is 10 percent how, and 90 percent why.

When your why is strong enough, you can accomplish

anything you set your mind to.

FIND YOUR WHY

I get asked (as do all the other leaders) how I run this business. It's always how, how, how. But I didn't realize when I started my business that it's not the *how* but the *why* that's important. This might be one of the most important things you can learn as you begin or continue your SendOutCards journey.

Why did you decide to build SendOutCards? What are your reasons? Most people say *money* or *time*, but it has to go deeper than that. Ask yourself this question—and take some time to think about it. Keep digging deeper. Here's a hypothetical example: Let's say I want to make $10,000 a month with SendOutCards. That's great, but why?

So I can quit my job. Why?

So I can spend more time with my family. Why?

Because I want to spend and enjoy every day with those I love, to travel with them, and to provide a good lifestyle for them.

That is a much stronger *why* than wanting to make $10,000 a month. When you break it down further and further, you get to the root of what you are really after in this business. Your *why* will probably be different from anybody else's, but the process of identifying it is one of the best things you can do.

Why? Because when you have days that you feel like quitting (I'll get to that in another chapter), you look at your *why*; if it is strong enough, you move forward. If it's not, you've sabotaged yourself. Finding your *why* as you begin your SendOut-Cards business will help you develop deep roots anchoring you to this business, no matter what comes your way. If you have been in awhile and don't have your *why* in front of you every day, now is the time to find it.

My *why*:

• So no one can ever tell me what to do. I make my own choices.

• So I can create financial freedom for myself and my family so we never have to worry about money.

• So I can buy a plane and travel the world, enjoying amazing experiences with friends, family, and team members.

• So I can provide for my family the same lifestyle that my parents created for my brother and me.

• So I can be the go-to guy, the one who always treats, the one who helps others when they are in need.

• So I can look in the mirror every day and be proud of the person I am.

I also asked some of the top leaders for their *why* behind SendOutCards and have included their answers here. These are all written in their words. You will see a wide variety, and your *why* can change as you progress through the business.

JIM PACKARD

I'm following a path that I was led to through God. I have had signs pointing in this direction for a number of years. I don't want my wife Sherry to ever have to compromise when she's buying something for herself. I want to prove to my family and myself that I could start another business and be successful. I want to fund a foundation scholarship called the Packard Foundation for Winthrop High School. I want to buy a family compound on the coast of Maine for generations to come.

JEFF PACKARD

Why am I doing SendOutCards? First of all, I love it. In the beginning I got into it because I wanted to make some extra money. I just set goals for my promotions and have been working with my team to achieve them. I enjoy SendOutCards because we have a cool product, and I like recognizing people for the talents they have. I believe we all need people in our lives that see us better than we are. That, to me, is network marketing.

The leadership traits you pick up are tremendous because you are building a team. The only way to build a successful team is to be a good leader. So this is why I continue to do Send-

OutCards—because I love people and helping them achieve greatness.

DAVID FREY

My *why* statement is "I'm building a successful SendOut-Cards business so that when I'm not here, my family will be financially secure." *David has a health issue that gives life and meaning to his* why *statement whenever he reflects on it.*

DEMARR ZIMMERMAN

I was working out of town in New Mexico. I lived out of a suitcase for three weeks out of the month. I had four kids and a wife I hardly saw, and I wanted to be home. I was in debt up the ying-yang and had to work just to pay my debts. I wanted to be free from debt. I was making good money, but I didn't have much time freedom.

I was living the American fake dream. I wanted to be home! I wanted to be with my family! I wanted to sit down at night with a home-cooked meal and ask my wife and kids face-to-face how their days had been. I was tired of long-distance relationships with my family.

JORDAN ADLER

Have fun, be free, and do good in the world!

KATHY PAAUW

I am providing for our family so my husband and I have the financial freedom to spend our time however we want. I am teaching people to take 100 percent responsibility for their own lives and am offering hope to those who have felt hopeless. I am helping them follow their dreams. I am promoting peace. I live in servitude, gratitude, and with love and compassion for those I encounter. My family is living in our dream home on the Kirkland waterfront. Doug and I are traveling the world with family and friends as we enjoy relaxation, having new experiences, learning about new cultures, and making new friends.

TOMMY WYATT

Buckle up! Growing up, my father worked for IBM, and I moved four times in a seven-year period. Each time I had to make new friends and start over. The final time, as a junior in high school moving from California to Connecticut, I got pissed off. I became a rebel and started cutting school and getting into trouble. I ended up graduating (by a miracle) 364th out of 364. My parents paid for college, but I never went to class. For six years! From age 17 to 23, I had 25 different jobs. Quit most of them—got fired a lot too. I just *hated* being told what to do. That's my main personality characteristic. At 23 I got a low-paying job as a sportswriter and was there for 10 years. Finally, I had found my voice (or so it seemed).

Both my little brothers graduated college and went on to become very successful financially. Though I was also successful, I was broke. Found network marketing at age 33 and built a business into seven countries. Even then, my *why* was the same as it is now: To show the world that even though I was an underdog, I could still achieve massive success.

CURTIS LEWSEY

Going through college I had no extra money, so when I graduated all I wanted to do was make a lot of money. Things changed a bit one week after I graduated. The night before my first conference baseball championship, my dad and my sister walked into my hotel to inform me that my brother Silas had passed away. He died in a freak dirt bike accident. I was only 21, and I began to think of life a little differently. Money was no longer my number-one burning desire; instead, it was being able to live the rest of my life as I wish to. I began to think *why* does college have to be *the* four best years of your life—why can't it be four *of* the best years of your life? I told myself I will create a lifestyle without limitations for myself and my family.

DIANE WALKER

My *why* started years ago, when I was fed up with being a corporate slave. I wanted to be free not only to break out of that type of life, but to help others do the same. I accomplished that prior to SendOutCards, but it was *not* easy, and while I was making a better income than in my "job" world, it was hard to duplicate and help others do the same. I sent cards to my own customers, but I did it the old way—by hand.

When I saw SendOutCards for the first time, I thought it was the coolest idea I'd ever seen, and I could see where it would help me in my other business. I started sharing with others I knew who could use it as well, and the smart ones saw it too, and it started growing. I *love* SendOutCards, and I see it as something I can do to give others a chance to reach their dreams. I believe in the company and the system, and I can feel good about sharing it and helping others. I want to change the world and help others out of the difficult economy or their own struggles.

I was raised in the old way of getting a "job" with benefits and staying there until you die or retire. I raised my kids that way too, and I'm sorry for that now. I know that world no longer exists, but my kids seem to think it does and are stuck in it. I want to share and help others get out of that mindset and just make a difference. I don't have any major *why* like the guys who want planes or big houses or cars. I really have all the material things I need. I have two nice cars, and I don't have to get up unless I want to. I can and do travel. All those things are great, but I want to give something back to others and teach them that they can accomplish things too.

BOB AND BETTY ANN GOLDEN

We have learned over the course of 40 years of marriage that the most important things to us are our family, friends, each other, and good health to enjoy it all. We saw our parents work hard for a living and then struggle financially after they retired. When we were introduced to SendOutCards, it was at a pivotal time in our lives. From the outside, it appeared that we had it all. But from the inside, the story in our minds had us believing that we had no time to enjoy those most important things. We were stuck on the merry-go-round of making a living and could not get off.

Thanks to SendOutCards, we now have new stories in our minds. We not only want to be here for our family, our grandchildren and each other, we want to be able to do what we want, when we want, in the style we want and most importantly, to share it with those we choose to share it with. Our *why* is to provide residual financial freedom for our family and future generations to come. We now have an even greater *why*: To be a part of a movement of bringing love, hope and dreams to many by creating a foundation dedicated to educating children worldwide, coupled with the same personal development we learn at the Treat 'em Right seminars. How awesome our world will be when more children grow up knowing their greatness within. Now that's a "golden life!"

DAVE AND LORI SMITH

I believe a person's *why* changes constantly—until they find the *why* that makes them cry. I first started SendOutCards to get to $4,000 of extra income per month just to see if I could. Then I decided I was doing it to get out of contracting, a roller-coaster ride I had been on for 20 years. Then I was excited about doing SendOutCards to be able to travel with Lori and relax a bit. Lately I have been excited about the possibilities of helping others get what they want out of the SendOutCards experience.

The *why* that makes me cry is to have the time and money to allow each one of my grandkids to experience "Grandma's Ami" with Lori and me. A few years back Lori and I went to Miami for a weekend. When we came home, we gave a little bag of seashells to Bridgee, our four-year-old granddaughter.

She asked Lori where she got them, and Lori said, "In Miami." A few weeks later, as people asked Bridgee where she got the seashells, she would say Grandma brought them home from her Ami. Bridgee's dad said, "Don't you mean Miami?" but she said, "No, Dad, it's not your Ami; it's Grandma's Ami." At that moment we decided to take all our grandkids on a special trip to Miami on their fifth birthday. Bridgee is now almost seven, and she still talks about Grandma's Ami.

So my *why* is having the time and money to experience Grandma's Ami with all my grandkids. That one sentence in my mind represents a lot more than just a quick trip to Miami, and that's just the beginning.

SETTING YOUR GOALS WITH SENDOUTCARDS

My original goal with SendOutCards was to make the same amount in SendOutCards as I was making in my current job, which was about $2,000 a month. My next goal was to double it, and then double it again. I didn't have a timeline, and it's up to you whether you want to put a timeline on your goals.

Some of my goals have timelines, and others I just write down and see what happens. Our family has been setting goals for a long time. Every year since I was in fifth grade, my father has asked my brother and me for one Christmas present each year—our goals in writing. My goals and how I write them have evolved over the last 20 years, but each year I look forward to the process.

For SendOutCards I recommend writing your monthly and yearly goals and keeping them in front of you—look at them at least twice daily. You can find the form we use for our SendOutCards goals at www.thepackardteam.com; the password is *thepackardteam*. The monthly goals my father, brother, and I keep track of are:

1) Points (using the Scorecard)
2) Gift account walkthroughs—personal or three-way
3) Collecting one story a week
4) Working on personal growth

Once you have the goals written down, you need to have an action plan to achieve them. What can you do every day to help you move towards your goals? Start right away. If your goal is ten new card senders or ten new distributors this month, what actions do you need to take to reach that goal? If you start keeping track, you will know your numbers.

On average, one out of three people I introduce to SendOutCards chooses to get involved. Your numbers might be higher or lower, but when you are getting started in this business, you make up in numbers what you lack in skill. You will gain more confidence as you go. If you hand out 30 magazines a month or have 30 people send a card and watch the DVD, you will enroll new distributors.

Again, it goes back to the Scorecard and focusing on your *actions*—and the results will follow. However, if you don't know what your monthly and yearly goals are, you are just going through the motions. Write down your goals and keep them in front of you. Share them with your accountability partner and your upline. Trust me, your upline will *want* to help you reach your goals!

CHAPTER 3

Commitment and Focus

One reason so few of us achieve what we truly want is

that we never direct our focus; we never concentrate our

power. Most people dabble their way through life, never

deciding to master anything in particular.

TONY ROBBINS

So you have decided to build a SentOutCards business. Are you ready for a wild ride? Nothing worthwhile is ever easy, but it is *worth it*. Like Tony Robbins says in the quote above, too many people dabble, never focusing on what they want, or they always change their focus. A couple of analogies will help you understand how this business works.

GET IN LINE, STAY IN LINE

Have you ever stood in line at a buffet? You get in the back of the line and slowly move forward. You finally reach the plates, then the salad, then the main courses, and then the dessert. Finally, you get to sit down and enjoy it.

Here is what happens to a lot of people in any home-based business: They get in line, they are slowly moving forward, and they finally reach the salad. But they get distracted. The buffet next door smells really good. You know it took you some time to get to the front of the line and start enjoying it a little, but you really have an urge for something different—plus the line isn't moving fast enough. You get out of line and go next door.

What happens next? You get in the back of the line and start all over again. I see this happen to so many people in our business. They get in, they start to gain some momentum, and then they jump ship. They never get to the good stuff. They never get to enjoy what they are working for because they believe the grass is always greener somewhere else. Get the message? Get in line and stay in line.

This business requires commitment and focus. You have decided to work SendOutCards as a business. You have written down your *why*, you have your accountability partner, goals, and an action plan, and you are getting to work. Once you commit to something, stay focused on the journey! If you follow through with your plans and learn as you go, you will succeed. If you aren't seeing the level of success you want quickly enough, the holdup is not the company or your upline—it is *you*. If you go to another company, you will repeat your same old ways and probably never get to the dessert portion of your company. When you finally decide that *this is it*, the right people and circumstances will come into your life. Those who are always looking for the next biggest thing or the next ground-floor opportunity will always be chasing their tails. Find a company you love and make a decision. Focus on your goals and your action plan and get to work! You don't want to be a jack-of-all-trades and a master of none.

DON'T START AND STOP

Not only is focus and commitment important in this business, but also *consistency*—it's one reason I have been successful. At one of our conventions, Jordan demonstrated the importance of not starting and stopping in business. He talked about taking action daily to grow your business. The room was divided into two large sections. The demonstration was simple: One person on each side stood up at a time, and that person touched two people. Once those two people were touched, they stood up and each touched two more people, and so on and so forth until the entire section was standing.

The difference was one side continued, while the other had to stop when Jordan said so. He only said, "Stop," a few times and only for a second or two. But the difference was astounding. By the time the uninterrupted side of the room was completely standing, only one-third of the other side was. This demonstrates the importance of continuous action and gaining momentum.

Compound interest has been called the eighth wonder of the world. Most people don't realize a business is just like compounding interest. Each day you do something to grow your business, the magic of compounding is working for you. Each day you don't do something, the magic of compounding is working against you. If you are supposed to eat an apple a day, you can't eat 30 apples on the last day of the month to make up the previous 29 skipped days. If you double a penny every day for 30 days, do you know how much money you have?

It's incredible what this momentum creates for you in your business. Take a standard sheet of paper. Fold it eight times, the maximum number you can fold it. You see how thin the paper still is. How thick would it be if you were physically able to fold it 50 times? All the way to the sun. Fifty-one times? All the way to the sun and back. That is the power of geometric progression, and network marketing is the same way. The challenge is most of us never get past seven or eight folds.

RUN THE NUMBERS

Let's take an average leader in our business. Assume this person has been in for one year, has 300 distributors, and is earning $3,000 to $5,000 a month—a pretty good goal. If the business doubles in size every year, the number of reps goes from 300 to 600, 600 to 1,200, 1,200 to 2,400, 2,400 to 4,800, 4,800 to 9,600, 9,600 to 19,200, 19,200 to 38,400, and 38,400 to 76,800.

You get the picture. The first few years are obviously not as lucrative; however, after eight years of building the business, if the magic of compounding is working for this leader, he or she will go from 300 reps to nearly 80,000 and increase in salary from $3,000 to $100,000 or $200,000 a month! Would you stick with a company and keep your focus if you knew the power of compounding and your daily actions? To get big results, you have to think big.

The first two to four years, you are just holding on. Think long-term and know that compounding is working for you.

CHAPTER 4

Network Marketing vs. Traditional Job

Ninety-five percent of network marketers who stay with

one company reach the top level of the pay plan in ten

years.

MARK YARNELL

For those of us with little or no network-marketing experience, it is important to know how we are paid and how this compares to the traditional nine-to-five job most people maintain. When I joined SendOutCards, all I knew was if I enrolled and coached a new customer or new distributor, I would get paid. As my team grew, I knew my residual income, which is based on the number of cards and gifts purchased, would grow as well. I didn't want to know the details of the pay plan; I didn't need to. All I wanted to know was the basics, and that is all you should teach your team as they begin their SendOutCards journey. Trying to understand every detail of the compensation plan before you do any work will slow your growth in this business.

How you get paid in a traditional job is very simple: You work an hour, you get paid for that hour. You are trading your time for money. You can expect your income to be based on the work you do and hours you put in. You are on a salary or get paid hourly, so there are no surprises. However, there is one major challenge to this: There is usually an income ceiling of some kind, unless you are straight 100 percent commission sales (which isn't a job; that would mean you are self-employed).

When I joined SendOutCards, I thought of my income in annual terms—$30,000 a year, $50,000 a year, or $100,000 a year. However, as soon as I got in and saw the potential, I started thinking of my income in terms of monthly income. In what other business can your previous yearly income become your monthly income? How cool is that?

The challenge is most people never get the ball rolling or start seeing those checks. Remember you have to get in line and stay in line to get to the good stuff! And in the beginning you don't get paid in proportion to the effort you put in. You are going to be doing a lot but not seeing a lot of checks (this is not always the case but is the tendency). However, the tradeoff is that once you are in for awhile and build a good team, you get paid way more than you should for doing less work. Sounds like a pretty good tradeoff! In the beginning you might do some activity and not see the result for months down the road; you have to be prepared for that.

Here is my analogy for having a job versus having a network-marketing business:

Traditional Job:
Work, work, check. Work, work, check. Work, work, check. Eight hours a day, 40 hours a week for 40 years, and then you get to retire and enjoy your life. Sounds like a prison sentence to me.

Network Marketing:
Work, work, work, work, check, work, work, work, work, work, check, work, check, work, check, check, check, work, big check, vacation, check, vacation, check, work, vacation. It all equals more work in the beginning but bigger rewards as you stay in line.

The beautiful thing about this business is it can be worked part-time to achieve these results. When people ask me if I am full-time, I say I am, but it's not the traditional full-time people are used to. Some days I might work eight hours, some I might work two—it just depends. But I know as I keep the ball rolling, the rewards continue to come. You have to get through the first year knowing your work output might not equal the pay you are seeking. It's okay and it's normal. Stick with it because good things will happen in the long run.

CHAPTER 5

Follow the Leader

Management is doing things right; leadership is doing

the right things.

PETER DRUCKER

BE A PRODUCT OF THE PRODUCT

Have you ever had people try to sell you something, and when you ask how they like it, the response is, "Well, I don't use it"?

Interesting. How can you represent a product you aren't excited about and aren't using? In SendOutCards you can't deny that we have one of the best products available. If you are not taking advantage of that product as much as you should, start now. We teach sending one heartfelt card every day and one gift a week—those are the minimums. It's up to you if you want to do the minimum.

From the beginning I sent a ton of cards, and when we came out with gifts, I immediately started sending them on a regular basis. The reason for doing this? It gives you credibility. It creates stories. And every card and gift you send is like a little prospecting soldier working for you. The more cards and gifts you send, the more you are into this business.

If you are reading this, you're not the type of person to do the minimum. You want more and deserve more. The leaders in this business all send a lot of cards—just ask them. Be a product of the product, and you will get even more excited about this business. And make sure you teach this principle to your team!

YOUR TEAM WILL DO WHAT YOU DO, NOT WHAT YOU SAY

Your team will only move as fast as you move. When you are getting started, it will feel like you are working the business by yourself, which will be discussed later. However, you have to keep your personal production up. I average about 30 walkthroughs a month—sometimes more, sometimes less— but that is pretty typical. I average 50 to 60 points on my Daily 8 Scorecard. I enroll eight to twelve card senders a month, both distributors and customers. My team continues to grow. I have found that when I slow down on my personal production, my team slows down. When I keep my personal production high, my team follows. Your team will do what you do, not what you say. Do you attend the conference calls? Do you use the tools SendOutCards gives you? Do you attend the Super Saturday events? Do you go to the Treat 'em Right Seminars?

Do you get to the Annual Convention? Stay connected! These are critical steps to building your business, but you would be surprised how few people get involved and get plugged in. Every day ask yourself, *If my team did what I did today, how would my business look?* The speed of the leader is the speed of the team. Get into action, and your team members will follow you to the top.

WHAT HAS SENDING CARDS DONE FOR YOU?

Before I joined SendOutCards, I probably sent about ten cards a year. A few thank you cards, a few birthday cards and that was about it. I knew it was something I should be doing more often, but I never got around to it. Once I joined Send-OutCards, I heard the philosophy of one heartfelt unexpected card each day. Now, since we have gifts, it's a card a day and a gift a week. That is the average. I probably send three to five heartfelt cards a day and two to three gifts a week. The more you send out the more you get back!

Once I heard this philosophy, I had to do two things. First, start looking for opportunities to send cards and gifts. Second, take some time every day and just think about the people in my life and who needs to get a card from me. When all is said and done in this life, and when I look back, I know the relationships I develop will mean the most to me. Picking one person a day to send a card to only helps strengthen those relationships. Many days I find myself sending multiple cards.

If you have a few people that you think of, don't just send one! If you get to the gifts page and are prompted to send them a gift, send it. Act on it!

WHAT SENDING CARDS HAS DONE FOR ME

Life moves quickly. Most of us are so busy that we never stop and smell the roses. Every day, when I sit down and just reflect for a few minutes about the people in my life, I focus, I am present, and I feel a sense of gratitude for the relationships I have in my life. Sending cards and gifts help me celebrate those relationships. When I send unexpected and heartfelt cards and gifts, it puts me in a positive mindset. My energy is stronger. I slow down and enjoy the moment. We talk about personal development in this business. Sending out heartfelt cards every day is part of it, because it gets your mind to a better place. What you send out is what you get back, and this activity is critical to getting your day off to a good start. Whenever I'm having a tough day, it's usually because I'm focusing too much on myself. When I catch myself in this attitude, I like to pause and reflect, and then reach out to someone who needs to hear from me with an encouraging word, card, gift - anything to make them feel better. Trust me, when you make someone else's day, your day will be much more fun.

I love looking for fun ways to send cards to people. I learned this lesson from DeMarr Zimmerman. I was at the BMW dealership getting my car serviced. I always go to the same person — Jennifer. Every time I am there she is in a good mood and helpful. I wonder how often she gets recognized for being great at what she does. I grabbed one of her cards, and asked her who her manager was. Immediately she was probably thinking, "is something wrong?" I didn't say much, just that I would like to have his name. When I got home, I sat down and created a card. I took a picture of me in front of my car, and put it on the inside, and addressed the card to the manager of the dealership. Here is what I wrote:

Dear David,

I just wanted to write you a quick note to let you know how much I enjoy working with Jennifer. Each time I bring my car in for service, she greets me with a smile and is ALWAYS positive. No matter what the problem, small or large, she is professional, courteous, and very good at what she does. I'm not sure how often she gets recognized for this, but she deserves it. Could you do me a favor? Could you give her this box of brownies on my behalf and let her know she is doing a great job, and that I really appreciate her? I appreciate it.

Have an awesome day!

Adam Packard

Instead of just sending the box of brownies to Jennifer, which would have been great, I wanted her to get a little extra recognition. So now, one card and gift has affected three people instead of two. Now when I go into the dealership they roll out the red carpet and treat me even better. Jennifer was so appreciative of the card, I don't think she will ever forget it. That card and gift made David's day, Jennifer's day, AND my day.

Too often we only hear complaints or what's wrong—send someone a card that recognizes them for what they are doing right. You will be blown away by the impact this has on you! In that previous story, Jennifer and David were affected by the card. But I would say it probably had the biggest effect on me. When I created the card, it put me in such a positive and appreciative state of mind. When I am grateful and I focus on what I have, I continue to be given more. When I focus on lack or what I don't have, there is more struggle. People ask me who is affected more by sending card—the sender or the recipient? I believe the sender is affected the most. It puts me in a great mindset of gratitude and appreciation, AND I get to enjoy the reaction from the receiver in a few days as well.

Stop asking yourself, "what's in it for me?" and get beyond yourself. Will sending cards help you grow your business? Absolutely. Is that the main focus and the main reason why you are sending these cards? Absolutely not. If you come from a place of trying to "get" something when you are sending cards, it can have the opposite effect. When you take yourself and your expectations out of it and just enjoy the process, you will be genuine and sincere with your cards and it will help you create stories—stories that inspire and bring out the best in everyone.

CHAPTER 6

Be a Master of How You Spend Your Time

One cannot manage too many affairs; like pumpkins in the

water, one pops up while you try to hold down the other.

CHINESE PROVERB

How you spend your time in this business will dictate how well you do. Whether you are putting 30 minutes a day into this or are going at it full-time, focusing your efforts on the best activities will lead to the best results.

CREATE YOUR STORY

What is your story? Why did you join SendOutCards? You should have already come up with your *why*; once you have this, you need to share it with the people you introduce to SendOut-Cards. People relate to stories. If you tell someone you got into SendOutCards to make money, that's okay. If you tell them you were tired of working for someone else and you wanted to find a way to stay home with your kids so you can enjoy every day more, you've got a more powerful story. Create your own story and share it with others.

ARE YOU BUSY, OR ARE YOU PRODUCTIVE?

I could spend hours talking about this topic. I see so many different activities from distributors. Truth be told, there are only a handful of activities that help move your business *forward*. There are a lot more activities that keep you treading water. It is my goal to keep my distributors productive, focusing on those activities that will help them build the business the fastest way possible. I hope to shed some light on what to focus on and what to avoid. How you spend your time in this business is critical, especially if you are working it part-time.

WHAT ARE THE INCOME-PRODUCING ACTIVITIES FOR SENDOUTCARDS?

If you follow The Daily 8, you are on the right track. I focus on a few activities, and I encourage my team to do the same. Obviously you are going to be sending cards and gifts (refer to the last chapter if you are stuck on that one!). When I started my business, my focus was on building my contact manager—always having people in my pipeline to talk to. You don't want to run out of contacts, but you are in luck: There are people *everywhere*! Don't take this for granted. If you have a big contact manager but never contact anyone, it's like buying a treadmill and not using it. You won't get in shape by buying a treadmill and letting it sit in your house, and you won't build a Send-

OutCards business by building your contact manager and not contacting the people in it.

Once you have built your list, focus on contacting and showing people SendOutCards. This could mean having them watch the DVD, inviting them to a presentation, or having them do a walkthrough or demo. Exposures, exposures, exposures. Building your contact list and getting in touch with those people are the big steps—obviously follow-up is key, as well as training, but if you don't accomplish the first two steps, you will never get to follow-up and training.

Continue to build your contact manager. Keep your pipeline full and show SendOutCards to as many as you can. You will get to the point where people start calling *you* to get started—then you really get to choose who you want to work with. If you find yourself chasing or trying to push people off the fence, go back to building your contact manager and contacting new people. As Super Dave Smith says, send cards and show others how to send cards. That's it.

TIME-SAVING TIPS

To get the most out of your day, you need to have an idea of what holds most people back. There are plenty of time-wasting activities. When you make the decision to work SendOutCards, block off time every day as your SendOutCards time and stick to it. Eliminate the distractions and find a place where you can totally focus on your business. Adopt a few ground rules:

Rule Number One: Turn off your e-mail. People have become so glued to their e-mail that they never get anything done; they are always responding and replying. If you are working Send-OutCards for an hour or two, turn it off. Chances are very slim that you will receive an "urgent" e-mail during that time. It's tough to do but very liberating. I currently check my e-mail twice a day and never first thing in the morning or before I go to bed.

Rule Number Two: Screen incoming calls. I tell new distributors not to answer incoming calls during SendOutCards time, unless they recognize the number as a prospect they've been trying to reach. If you are making outbound phone calls and doing presentations, wait until after you have completed those tasks to return calls. Five-minute conversations with distributors or friends turn into 30-minute visits, and then you have lost crucial time in building your business. If you find yourself having long conversations with distributors, make sure your chats are productive. If someone calls you and starts talking SendOutCards, ask one question: "How is your SendOutCards business going?" If the response is anything other than SendOutCards, politely let the person know you have a call you have to make.

WORK WITH THOSE WHO DESERVE IT, NOT THOSE WHO NEED IT

I had to learn this lesson as I built my business. The challenge is, we want everyone to be successful. Not everyone you bring into SendOutCards will want the same things you want. You have to get really good at deciding who you spend time with. Those who deserve your time are the ones calling you—they are doing the work, they are signing people up, they are attending the calls, they attend events, and they are plugged into SendOutCards. Those who need it are the ones you *think* could be really good. So you keep calling them and tracking them down, trying to get them to work the business. This will drive you crazy in the long run, and your business will grow very, very slowly. Jordan Adler is an expert at where he spends his time, so his group grows quickly. The longer you are in SendOutCards, the more you will recognize the difference between these two types of people.

YOU CAN'T BE FRIENDS WITH EVERYONE IN YOUR DOWNLINE

We all have a desire to love and be loved, but in your network-marketing business, you can't be everything to everybody. As much as you want those on your team to love you and be your friend, you have to remember you are their business partner first and their friend second. As much as I would like everyone to be my friend in my group, I know that will probably never be the case. Being a leader in this business means telling people what they *need* to hear, not what they *want* to hear. I have no problem calling people out if they start complaining and I know they are not doing the work. Your team will appreciate your honesty and your leadership. Your goal is to help them build a big business, and they need to hear the truth from you, even if it hurts initially.

GET PEOPLE STARTED BUT DON'T DO IT FOR THEM

I always tell new team members, "You are in business for yourself, but not by yourself." As the upline, you need to be there for support and coaching, but there's a fine line between helping people get started and doing the work for them. Your goal is to get your new team members started as quickly as possible. Help them set up their site, show them The Daily 8, give them a few action items, and see when they get back to you. When you give your new distributors the 72-Hour Challenge, you will find out very quickly who wants to work this business.

If you find you are always the one tracking down team members and motivating them to get going, you will burn yourself out trying to get them to act. It's like pushing a rope—it doesn't work. You can only carry so many people on your back, and I don't want to carry anyone! My goal is to teach someone to fish, not give them a fish. When you give people the tools and then allow them to take care of themselves, you have less stress in your work and a faster-growing business. If you don't have anyone who is a builder yet, you have two choices: Sign up more distributors or try to convert your current distributors to business builders. I have done both, and trying to get a distributor to become a builder is like trying to figure out why the sun sets in the west. I wouldn't spend much time on it! Go out and sponsor new reps, and you will find those who want to build.

CHAPTER 7

It's All You in the Beginning

No great achievement is possible without persistent

work.

BERTRAND RUSSELL

The idea of persistence goes back to the difference between the traditional job and network marketing—knowing that it's going to require a bit of a push initially, and to compound that, not everyone you sign up as a distributor will work SendOutCards like you are. The reality is that out of ten people you sign up, three will do absolutely nothing, three will do very little, three will work it part-time, and one will work it like you are. It's a numbers game.

When I first started, the majority of prospecting was done by leading with the service—showing someone how to send a card, and then, "oh, by the way," there is a business opportunity as well. I signed up a lot of distributors, but they were really wholesale customers with a distributor account. Because of this, it took a lot of distributors before I found some who really want to work the business. So if you feel like you are working this all by yourself in the beginning, that's okay and to be expected. It might take you 30 distributors, it might take you 100, or it might be the first person you sign up, but you will find business builders if you persist. The key is to persist. Are you going to give up if you have 30 distributors and no one is working? It's your decision, but it's normal to feel like you are doing all the work at the outset, so keep going! If you lead with the opportunity and the business, you will attract more who want to build the business. Most top network marketers lead with the opportunity rather than the product—at least that's the way for those making the most money. It's different with SendOutCards. We have such a strong product, but we also have an amazing opportunity. It's your choice: You can lead with the system and the service and attract a lot of customers, or you can lead with the business and the opportunity and attract more business builders. Find three new distributors, give them the 72-Hour Challenge, and help them become a Success Unit. If only one of the three takes you up on it, go find new distributors and keep building Success Units.

GET TO SENIOR MANAGER

When I enroll a new distributor, I always tell them the first goal is to get to Senior Manager. If you are already a Senior Manager or above, congratulations. If you aren't, get to work! Senior Manager is where the money starts to kick in, so I encourage you to put your head down and get to Senior

Manager as fast as you can. You can either sign up a handful of reps and help them bring in a few more, or you can bring them all in yourself, but please don't wait for your team to do something. Go out there and get it done yourself. If you show SendOutCards to 100 people, you should be a Senior Manager. It's as simple as that. It's up to you how fast you want to get there. As my good friend Tommy Wyatt says, when you tell your team members to get to Senior Manager as fast as they can, they are going to ask how fast *you* got there. If you get there fast, your team will follow suit. People have made Senior Manager in less than two weeks; for some it takes two years. It's up to you.

When I saw that I needed 24 people to get to Senior Manager, I thought, *Wow, I only need 24.* Many distributors look at that and think, *Wow, I need 24? That's a lot.* You get what you focus on, and it's all about perspective. Remember, the speed of the leader is the speed of the team.

I love asking new distributors and Senior Managers, "Are you willing to get to $10,000 a month in income if you have to do it working by yourself?" The answer may be how much someone wants it. You will probably attract a lot of business builders, and you won't have to get to $10,000 on your own, but knowing you will do whatever it takes to get there will only make you stronger.

YOUR TEAM WILL BE LIKE A BASKET OF FRUIT

Everyone is different. Some people will sign up one person a year, some one a month, some one a week, some one a day. Your challenge is to help them along without trying to get those who do one a year to make the leap to doing one a day. It is up to them to improve, with your leadership and guidance, but trying to get people to increase production is challenging. You are better off looking where you found distributors who are bringing in one rep a week—or, even better, one rep a day—and going out and prospecting for new distributors like them.

CHAPTER 8

Have Fun!

People rarely succeed unless they have fun in what they

are doing.

DALE CARNEGIE

One of the reasons my father, brother, and I have had success with SendOutCards is that we *love* what we do. We have fun doing it. But you would be surprised how serious people get when they work this business.

Whether you are busy building a SendOutCards business or just getting started, you are obviously doing it for a reason. A lot of people join because they don't like what they are currently doing or want to improve what they are doing. SendOutCards is a fun business. Who doesn't love greeting cards and gifts (and making money)? If you are not having fun with SendOutCards, find a way to make it fun. Get around other distributors who are enjoying the business and find out what they do to make it more fun. This key to success is so easy, so start enjoying this business!

You attract people very similar to you to your business. So take a long, hard look in the mirror: Do you want more of you in your business? Be excited about this company and where it is headed—enthusiasm is contagious! People want to join a company that is growing and has a good product, but they also want to do something they will enjoy.

Do you believe my father has fun doing this business? Once you've heard him speak at a seminar, you will have no doubt why he is successful in SendOutCards. He enjoys the work, but it doesn't feel like work. He makes games out of it. He has fun with people. He doesn't take himself too seriously. Why would someone want to join you in a business if you weren't having a good time doing it?

Even though there are lots of business opportunities out there, I don't believe there's a simpler, more fun company to join. I help people start their own greeting card business. I only get checks and greeting cards and gifts in the mail. What do you get? If you want to get checks and greeting cards in the mail, let me show you what I do! Our business is fun and easy, and it's time to treat it like that.

DESPERATION REEKS!

One thing I learned in this business is you can't say the wrong thing to the right person or the right thing to the wrong person. Your goal is not to "sign people up." Your goal is not to "close" someone. This is not sales. This is network marketing, and there is a *huge* difference. You are paid in direct proportion to people you help get started. The more you stress about people joining, the more you are pushing people away.

Have you ever *tried* to sign someone up and been pushed away? Are people not returning your phone calls? Remember, there is a fine line between follow-up and stalking. If you feel like you are chasing people down, *you are*!

My approach is fun, low key, and low pressure. I don't try to sign people up. My goal is to show them what we have, to give them all the information they need, and to let them decide if and when they are ready to join. Trust me, if you *need* people to sign up, they can sense it. People can sense desperation, and if you are in SendOutCards to sign someone up for a quick buck, your business will not grow like you want it to. People do not like being forced into making decisions.

If you ease your grip, making it your goal to simply expose people to SendOutCards, your results will be better. Let go of your obsession for signing people up, and you will most likely sign up more people. Signing someone up is just the beginning; to sponsor someone is to be responsible for that person. Your job doesn't *end* with sponsorship—it is just beginning!

COLLECT STORIES EVERY DAY

Founder and CEO Kody Bateman says life is a collection of stories. It truly is, and we have the best mechanism to collect them. Remember, you have to be a product of the product first—that way you can start collecting stories.

If you are newer and don't have any stories yet, get to a few events and borrow other stories (don't pretend they are yours!). Every time I show someone this business, I tell them the story of how and why I got started. If I'm talking to someone who works in a specific industry, I share a story that person can relate to. People love stories; they connect with them. A presentation without a story is like a baseball game without a home run—it's tolerable but not that exciting.

If you have been in SendOutCards for a little while and are making some money, I think it's great to share what the new income has done for you. I tell people my first goal in SendOutCards was to make as much part-time with this business as I was making in my full-time job. I accomplished that in about two months. From there, the story just got more and more exciting.

Any network-marketing business is a personal-growth business, and I'm going to talk more about personal growth coming up. But take a hard look at yourself and see where you can improve. How can you be better? You attract who you are, not who you want. If you want big-time people in your business, you have to become a big-time person, whatever that means to you.

Smile, laugh, enjoy conversations and meeting new people. Take genuine interest in someone else and take the attention off yourself. It's not about you—it's about your team. Enjoy the process more and more every day, collect stories, and have fun! Your checks will grow if you do.

CHAPTER 9

Frustration is a Reality

Never quit on a bad day.

JORDAN ADLER

If you just live by this quote and do the work, you will do just fine in this business. Every distributor, and even the top leaders, have been frustrated at some point in this business. It is human nature to get frustrated, but how we deal with it separates the champions from the quitters.

Just so you know, we *all* have bad days, bad weeks, even bad months. A lot of the top people have gotten to the point where they felt like giving up, only to take a strong look at their *why*, their vision of their business and the company, and then plow ahead.

For me, frustration is a worthless emotion, something I totally avoid. In my journal I wrote, "The only way I can feel frustrated is if I consistently accept the false idea that I can't do anything to resolve or improve the situation. Instead, I remember that I am resourceful, committed, and determined, and that if it's meant to be, I can make anything happen." When I feel frustrated, I read that and it gets me right back on track.

Keep your emotions in check. Remember, this is not a get-rich-quick program; it's a get-rich-slowly program! My first couple of years in the business, I really let my emotions get the best of me. On my good days I would be so excited, and on my bad days I felt like my dog just got run over. I learned there are certain things you can control and certain things you can't control. What I can't control is who comes into my business or when someone decides to sign up. What I can control is my reaction.

Do I get frustrated, or do I look at it differently? I used to get frustrated quite a bit, but I have learned that to see long-term success in SendOutCards, I have to look at every experience as a chance to learn and grow. Every experience is just a result; it's neither good nor bad. *Good* or *bad* are just labels we made up to put on things. My definitions of *good* and *bad* are probably different than your definitions.

If you get frustrated, where do you go? What do you do? How can you avoid that? I suggest when you are feeling down, go up—which means talk to your upline, your sponsor, or a leader—and let your mentor get you back on the right track. When you are feeling great, talk to your downline, your team, and pump them up. Don't reverse the two!

How you handle and deal with emotions in this business is key. Remember, it's about having fun! If people don't want to be around you because you are negative or argumentative, you will attract either the same type of person to your business or no one at all. Be careful! Ask yourself if people like being around you. Take a self-assessment. If your attitude and outlook are good, good people come into your life. Those who are always filled with drama only create more drama.

Keep your emotions neutral or positive as much as you can. Don't get too excited when things are great and don't get down when things are not going your way. Only you can control how you feel, and if you feel good no matter what comes your way, adopting an optimistic perspective, good things will come to you. The energy you put out comes back to you, so if you get frustrated, snap out of it! Frustration will not do good things for your business. Learn from it, grow from it, and become stronger.

STAY THE COURSE

CHAPTER 10

Don't Compare Your Business to Others

Don't compare yourself with anyone in this world. If you

do so, you are insulting yourself.

ALEN STRIKE

Trying not to compare my business to others has been a personal challenge. I always wondered what I was doing differently and why my business wasn't growing like others. We all want our businesses to grow faster—they never grow fast enough. The checks don't get bigger fast enough. Every SendOutCards distributor comes into this business with a different set of skills, a different list of contacts, a different agenda, a different mindset, and a different list of goals. How could any two businesses be exactly alike? It is impossible, and therefore impractical, to compare one business to another.

The skills you bring to SendOutCards are unique, and I've realized that all you can do is all you can do. I didn't have the great network Jordan built over the years. I didn't have experience in referral marketing like David Frey, or the sales skills Jim Packard has, or the Internet background of Diane Walker. But I had my own skills, and I knew the only way for my business to get better was for me to get better. The better you get in all areas—attitude, prospecting, leading—the more your team will grow. Recognize your strengths and capitalize on them. You have a unique set of skills no one else has. You can't be someone you are not, but you can be the best possible version of yourself.

I've learned to capitalize on my strengths, instead of trying to work on my weak areas. I've got skills in certain areas, and in some areas I'm lacking. But I know which areas of my business produce the best results, so that's what I focus on. I decided early on I was going to master certain areas of this business and certain skills, and you can do the same thing.

If you find yourself envious of others and their business or income, *stop*! Having an attitude of envy or jealousy will drive your goals further away. I am thrilled for the success of those who are growing groups quickly. Instead of being discouraged, I look for ways my team and I can improve, rather than knocking others down. I look to other leaders as people I can learn from and emulate. No one in this business is better than you. We all started with our very first distributor, just like you. Some started earlier and some had more contacts, but the point is to do the best you can with what you have and keep getting better. The leaders are there to support and guide you, but remember, they were once in your shoes too.

CHAPTER 11

Income Reflects Personal Development

Formal education will make you a living; self-education

will make you a fortune.

JIM ROHN

My first personal-development program was "The Day that Turns your Life Around" by Jim Rohn. My brother sent it to me as a gift when I was living in Denver, Colorado, working during the day as a golf pro and at night as a bartender. I was working about 80 hours a week and making about $3,000 a month. I thought that was pretty good at the time, and I enjoyed what I was doing, but inside I knew I had more potential—and I needed to find a way to tap into that. Listening to that first CD program changed my life, and I have been on a personal development journey ever since.

In 2004 I was offered an opportunity to work with my brother Jeff and the famous sales trainer and speaker Tom Hopkins. The pay wasn't great, but what we learned made the job one of the best things that ever happened to me. Jeff and I discovered what separated the successful from the unsuccessful. We gained more and more confidence as we spent time with Tom, learning about the industry of personal growth and self-improvement. Jeff and I were both hooked on self-improvement and have been ever since.

I truly believe your income is a direct reflection of your own personal development. It's when you work on yourself and improve yourself that your skills get better and everything in general improves. The top leaders are firm believers in working on yourself, and the company has incorporated personal development into one of the support activities of The Daily 8 training program.

The more I got into the business of network marketing, the more I realized we are really a personal development business with a compensation plan wrapped around it. Those who succeed the most are those who always improve themselves and apply what they learn.

Write down the last five books that you read. How long has it been? I read about one book each month, sometimes more, because I love challenging and working on myself. I also attend lots of personal development seminars, from Tom Hopkins and Tony Robbins to T. Harv Ecker and Loral Langemeier.

Guess what? I meet *amazing* people through these events. People who want to improve themselves are usually open to improving their income or finding a fun business, and as De-

Marr Zimmerman, our second Eagle in SendOutCards, says, "I just might have a solution for that!"

You might think, *Oh, I read* Beach Money *already,* or *I've read* Think and Grow Rich *before*. If you read it a few years ago, read it again. You will always be at a different point in your life with a new set of circumstances. I love re-reading some of my favorite books, including *The Power of Your Subconscious Mind*, *The 4-Hour Workweek*, *The Magic of Thinking Big*, or *The Greatest Salesman in the World*. Find a few favorites and read them once a year; each time you will pick up something new and relevant to your life today.

My personal development journey is never ending. After listening to my first CD program with Jim Rohn, I decided if I ever saw a program, seminar, or book I wanted, I would purchase it and apply the lessons within. I knew an investment in myself was the best investment I could make. If we only use 10 percent of our potential, can you imagine the possibilities? The human brain is amazing, and we haven't even come close to tapping the potential of what we can do and who we can be. For me it's constant and never-ending improvement. Every day in every way I am getting better and better. We are either growing or we are dying—I choose to grow.

The more you work on yourself, the better your skills will get. Not only that, your confidence will improve. You attract better people into your business. You have more fun, you make more money, you enjoy life more, and you feel challenged. You grow as a person, and you become the authentic you that has been covered up by the influences all around us. A better way is possible, and it starts by committing to lifelong personal growth and improvement.

CHAPTER 12

My $30,000 Lesson

Take time to gather up the past so that you will be able

to draw from your experience and invest them in the

future.

JIM ROHN

I have learned some expensive lessons in my SendOut-Cards journey. Some I can measure; others I can't. I am not here to tell you how to run your business, but I will share what I (unfortunately) did and why I would not do it again. Remember, these are lessons I learned—some more expensive than others—and if I can keep a few people from losing money, I am happy.

DON'T COME UP WITH NEW SYSTEMS

We have an incredible system. The tools you need are provided by the company—the gift account, the presentations—

everything you need is provided for you. These tools have been tested in the field, and they work. If SendOutCards leaders decide we need another system, they will implement it. This business is all about keeping things simple; the easier you can make it and the easier you can teach it to someone else, the faster your team will grow.

Jordan Adler's message since he joined SendOutCards has always been the same: The steps to building your business are simple. Send at least one card a day and a gift a week. Send at least one prospecting card with a DVD every day. Show at least one person our business and system every day through gift account walkthroughs and DVD presentations. If you listen to his calls, you will hear his message over and over again. The result? He has the fastest-growing organization. Why? Because the message is clear, concise, simple, and consistent. What message are you giving your team? Sharing his is a good idea.

THE LESSON THAT CONTINUES TO COST ME

I will sum this up in two simple words: Don't stack. If you don't know what stacking is, I'm going to give a brief description and advise you not to do it.

Stacking is taking someone who is ready to sign up and placing them under someone else for no reason. When I was a Senior Manager, I was excited to get to Executive. So instead of waiting for others to work, I decided to push things along on my own. Someone I knew wanted to sign up, and I placed her under a buddy of mine so I could get the promotion I wanted. It didn't seem like a big deal at the time, but it has become and will become a bigger mistake.

The good thing is I learned from it, and I share this story with others so they can learn from it too. Our compensation plan is based on seven levels of residual income. Instead of this person being on my first level, I placed her on my third level. However, I also placed her in someone else's Manager group, not mine. So she was on the third level in my Senior Manager group, instead of my first level in both my Manager and Senior Manager group (for clarification on this consult your upline).

The upside? I got promoted faster. The downside? Just from that simple move, I am missing out on about $2,500 a month in income, from both bonuses and residual income. That one person now has a team of over 1,000 people growing every month. And that $2,500 a month is going to continue to grow. You might say, *Yes, but you got promoted faster.* True, but are you working this business to make money or to get rewarded for a promotion? If your goal is income, don't stack! Work the business the right way, and you will have a strong organization that grows faster and makes you more money. Those who stack don't make as much money because they are not taking advantage of the seven levels of our compensation plan. Oh, and as a side note, this woman's original manager is no longer working the business, but he still collects that $2,500 a month I could have received. Lesson learned!

CHAPTER 13

No Excuses!

You can make money, or you can make excuses, but you

can't make both.

UNKNOWN

If you have never started or operated your own business, you are in for some challenges. But if you know some of these challenges up front, you will be better prepared to handle them as they occur. Someone once told me that you can either make money or excuses but not both. I choose to make money, and I hope you do as well. Excuses are just self-imposed limits we use as an easy way out.

In this business you can't blame anyone or anything. The most common excuse I hear is, "My upline isn't helping me." I'm sorry, but this business is all you, and your upline is there for support, but even if it disappeared, you can still build a successful business. I never blamed my father or Jordan (my upline) for anything. And if I didn't have them as my upline and it was all up to me, I would still be successful. I made a decision to make this business happen, no matter what.

Write down exactly where you are in the business right now. What is your promotion level, your number of reps, and your income? Where you are is a direct reflection of what *you* have done—not what your team has or hasn't done, not how your upline has or hasn't helped you. Where you are right now is a direct reflection of you. The good news is you can always make it better, but you can never get into the blame game. All you have to blame is yourself. I always say if it's to be, it's up to me. I take personal responsibility for what my business and income look like.

Think of some of your excuses or some of your team's excuses:

I don't have time.
I can't do it.
I don't know where to find people.
My upline didn't help me.

The list goes on and on. Start asking yourself empowering questions, instead of making negative statements or excuses. Instead of saying, "I don't have time," ask yourself how you can *make* the time. Instead of saying, "I can't do it," tell yourself you can and are doing it—better and better every day.

It's up to you—you can either do what it takes to build the business, or you can come up with reasons why you aren't successful. The leaders in this business have become leaders by leaving excuses behind and doing what it takes to build teams. You can do the exact same thing.

Don't wait for the company to come out with the right tools or enhancements to the website. When I started this business, we didn't have half the tools we have now, and we still built huge businesses. The tools and products available today are so valuable, and if SendOutCards never came out with another tool or enhancement to help you build your business, you would be just fine. The basic action items are there for you, and you can do them *right now*. Don't wait, don't hold back, don't make any excuses. You are the leader of your team; get out there and lead by example.

CHAPTER 14

Big Picture vs. Little Picture

From the very beginning I saw this as a billion-dollar

company.

KODY BATEMAN

SendOutCards is a billion-dollar company in the making. When I started building this business, the company was doing about $5 to $10 million in sales. In 2009 we reached $47 million. From $5 million to $47 million is a huge jump, and with that comes challenges and growing pains. Guess what? From $47 million to one billion, we are going to have growing pains and challenges as well. My question to you is this: Do you focus on the billion-dollar greeting card company that we are, or do you focus on the little challenges along the way?

A perfect example of the importance of perspective occurred in early 2005 when SendOutCards leaders realized the compensation plan they initially started was not going to work long term for the company and its distributors. When they changed the comp plan, a lot of the distributors (who helped get the company started) were upset and not in favor of it. They argued, complained, and stopped working. They stalled. Jordan Adler, on the other hand, saw the change as a good thing and a step the company needed to take. He kept working the business and kept showing the system. As a result he has easily become the top team-builder in the business. When you focus on the positive, good things happen. When you dwell on the negative, you start moving backwards.

You will always face challenges—that's part of owning your own business. The beautiful thing about network marketing is the company deals with most of them for you. Your job is to find new customers and distributors to build the business. The job of the company is to provide vision and solutions to challenges that come up.

A COMPLAINT-FREE WORLD

A great book is *A Complaint Free World* by Will Bowen, who encourages readers to completely stop complaining—about anything—for 30 days. It is more challenging than it sounds. We don't realize how often we complain about little things. This book will challenge you to catch yourself, and I highly recommend reading it. It will make you a better person.

JUST IMAGINE

Imagine where this company is going to be in five years. Like Kody, I picture SendOutCards as a billion-dollar company, and I also picture myself with a team of hundreds of thousands of distributors. To get there I need to keep my eye on that big picture, not get distracted by the little stuff along the way. My job is to share my vision with my team and to sell the dream this business offers. Once I share that, we all go out and do what it takes to build the business. And I am not going to worry about the things I can't control because all I can do is lead my team by sharing the dream and let the smart people at SendOutCards help us get there. Trust me, Kody and the executive team are doing all they can to get this company to a billion dollars. I know Kody's dream when he started SendOutCards was not to get it to $47 million and 90,000 distributors and stop. His goal and vision is to help millions of people act on their promptings. *Millions.* That is a lot. I'll take a small percentage of that. Big picture versus little picture. Make sure you focus on what we have now and where we are going, not what we need and what we need to fix—that's a recipe for slow growth.

SOLUTION-ORIENTED VS. PROBLEM-ORIENTED

Life is 10 percent what happens to you and 90 percent how you react to it. When something comes up, how do you handle it? I used to get frustrated, worried, and stressed. Now I look at things that happen and ask myself, *What can I learn from this? How can I make it better? What is the best solution?* If I focus on the problems, I get more of them. I don't even see things as problems anymore; I just see things as results. The joy is in the journey, and the little challenges you have along the way are just the Higher Power's way of testing you to see how bad you want something. Many hit an obstacle and quit, but you won't do that. You'll take it head-on and make things better—and in turn, you and your business will grow.

At the Treat 'em Right Seminars, Kody tells us to focus on possibilities, not problems. What is possible for you and your team? What is possible for this company? The quality of your life is determined by the quality of the questions you ask yourself. Start asking yourself questions that focus on possibilities.

We are a part of something special. This company, its leaders, its vision, and what we are doing are all part of something bigger than ourselves. We have an obligation to share this message with the world. We have an opportunity to help people in so many ways. Don't get caught in a little-picture, problem-oriented world. It will not serve you well.

CHAPTER 15

The Power of *I Am*

The power of I am is that you already are.

KODY BATEMAN

Like I mentioned before, our family has always been a goal-setting family. I learned about *I am*'s for the first time at my first Treat'em Right Seminar in Scottsdale, Arizona, in July of 2005. *I am*'s are affirmation statements of who you want to be, what you want to have, or what you want to do. They are stated in present tense as if they are happening now. I have written and re-written my *I am* statements many times throughout my SendOutCards journey. They work. If you believe they don't work, you've got an *I am* working against you. What you say to yourself and how you feed your mind are keys to success or failure in SendOutCards. As Jordan Adler says, affirmations without action lead to delusion; action without affirmation leads to frustration.

I am statements put the Law of Attraction to work for you. They focus your mind on what you want and who you want to be. They give you positive self-talk. The more you repeat them to yourself, the faster they will come true because they become a part of you. To be effective, *I am*'s have to be stated in the positive, present tense; you have to say them with emotion, visualization, and belief that they have already come true. When you put feeling behind the words, your mind attaches to the feeling and will help guide you to take the actions that will make them come true. I have had many affirmations become reality, and I continue to write more and more. Here are my 2010 *I am* statements:

> *I am a Senior Executive*
> *I am in the best shape of my life and enjoy boundless energy*
> *I am enjoying my new penthouse loft at the Optima*
> *   with amazing views of the city*
> *I am lucky, I am grateful, I am blessed*
> *I am enjoying my new Cessna Corvalis 400 and flying*
> *   all over the world*
> *I am open to a loving and supportive relationship*
> *I am earning X a month in SendOutCards*
> *I am helping my team members achieve freedom in*
> *   both time and money*
> *I am a best-selling author and sought-after speaker*

Have any of these come true yet? Some of them I am living every day, and others are things I see in the very near future. I feel them, I see them happening, and I am excited.

Find something that gets you energized, write it down as an *I am* statement, and be prepared to attract good things into your life.

One of the best exercises I did last year was to write down my Be/Do/Have list. Instead of just writing down some of my goals, I thought, *I am going to write down a list of* everything *I want to be, do, and have.* It doesn't matter how unrealistic it seems; the key is getting your imagination and creativity working for you. Anything is possible. I encourage you to make your list. Here are a few things I wrote down:

Get my pilot's license
Learn Spanish
Travel to Australia
Learn to play guitar
Write and publish my first book
Own a plane
Give $1,000 away every day
Visit the seven wonders of the world
Learn to scuba dive

Create a list of over 100 things. Some may be material and some may be what you want to give back—your list is unique to you. Once you have your list together, go back and write a number next to each, representing the number of years in which you would like to accomplish the goal.

Mark down your one-year, three-year, five-year, ten-year, and 20-year goals. Then go through and circle your top four one-year items. Write down three action items to do right away and take one step towards them *immediately*.

Last year one of my goals was to get my pilot's license. I had always wanted to learn how to fly, but I never even considered getting my license—I didn't know it was possible. I wrote it down as one of my top four one-year goals. The next step was to take immediate action. I called a few friends who were pilots and had them point me in the right direction. I did my first "discovery flight" with Jim Pitman, and I was hooked. I started taking lessons and made that goal come true. Anything is possible when you start dreaming again.

I like nice things, but I'm more interested in travel and having good experiences. When I look back on my life, it's not about how big my house was or how nice my car was (although I do love fast cars!). For me it will be about the kind of person I was, the service I offered to others, the experiences I had, and the fun I enjoyed. It's about lifestyle design and waking up every day doing things I love.

Once you reach some of your goals, even if they are small, you have to celebrate! Celebrate little victories as well as big victories and give yourself a reward. To challenge myself this year, I not only have rewards attached to my goals, but I also have penalties for failing to achieve certain goals. I won't share what my penalties are, but they will hurt a lot! Tony Robbins says people work harder to avoid pain than they will to gain pleasure.

What is one of your goals? Write it down quickly. What is your reward if you reach it? What is your penalty if you don't? (Hint: Involve your friends and family with choosing a penalty; they can often help you find something you wouldn't think of on your own.)

Become a student of goal-setting, affirmations, and the power of your mind. The more you do, the more you will realize this business is not just about working through the activities. I encourage you to never stop your journey of learning because the moment you think you know it all, people will pass you by. There is always something more to learn.

STAY THE COURSE

CHAPTER 16

Sushi with Jordan

You know they don't cook that stuff.

JIM PACKARD
(REFERRING TO SUSHI)

We all have a circle of friends we spend more time with than others. Make a list of your five closest friends. Your income will be a direct reflection of who you spend the most time with. People are either a good influence and help us grow or a bad influence and hold us back. You might need to find a new circle of friends to get where you want to go. I was blessed because when I joined SendOutCards, my Dad and brother were both involved, and Jordan Adler was our upline. We were able to spend quality time with him, and since then I have surrounded myself with other leaders in the company, many of whom I call some of my best friends. If I'm making $100,000 a year, and I want to make $100,000 a month, I need to surround myself with people who will challenge me to get there.

Jordan and I have sushi whenever he and I are both in town. We both love sushi, but I really enjoy just being around someone who has great energy, great vision, and a clear idea of where he is going. I know I rub off on Jordan in positive ways too—or he would not spend time with me. Who do you know that you can take to dinner and befriend—someone who will challenge you and whom you will challenge? It doesn't have to be someone in SendOutCards; it can be anyone as long as he or she is helping you grow as a person.

I have more goals than being successful in SendOutCards. I want to be a professional at having fun. I know other people have done what I want to do, so all I need to do is find out how they did it and surround myself with other people who have the same goal. For me, beginning to become a pro at having fun has been as simple as reading one book, *The 4-Hour Work-week* by Tim Ferriss. I am having more fun now than I ever have. Find someone who has done what you want to do and learn from them. Model someone else. With SendOutCards, I saw someone who was successful, and said, "I'll just learn from him." Pick multiple areas of your life where you want to improve, and find role models and mentors in each one of them. People are willing to help; you just have to be willing to ask and eager to learn.

CHAPTER 17

Challenges

If it were easy, everyone would do it.

UNKNOWN

When you get into business for yourself, you are going to have many challenges. That is a fact. Here are just a few examples:

"He said he was going to sign up!"

"Why won't she call me back?" (that is in reference to the SendOutCards business, not my personal life)

"The card editor gave me an error message!"

"My card didn't get delivered."

"I was on hold way too long."

"My team is so lazy—they aren't doing anything!"

No matter what you do, things are going to come up. I can't tell you how many times I have had people promise they will sign up tomorrow and build the business. Tomorrow comes and goes with no new business builder. Never count people as new distributors until they are in the system! If I had a dollar for all the people who said they were going to sign up and never did, I would have at least a few bills in my wallet.

Challenges just test how much you want success with this company. Did you think it was going to be smooth sailing when you got started? Don't you think there would be more distributors if it were a piece of cake? The business is easy, but that doesn't mean you won't have challenges. I *love* challenges. Challenges just weed out the distributors who are not willing to do what it takes to build the business. They give me a sense of empowerment—like *Get out of my way; I know who I am, and I know where my team is going. Don't hold us back. We look at challenges as opportunites to learn, grow, and develop.* Challenges make life fun, and if everything were easy, life would be boring. It's all about perspective.

Teach this to your team, and they will look at things differently. If you want to be a leader in this business, smile when you face a challenge. Get excited. Find a solution. Learn from it. And never quit on a bad day; bad days happen when you look at challenges the wrong way. Remember where SendOutCards is going and ask yourself if you want to be a part of it. There is plenty of room at the top, and the view is great, but few will make it. Will you be one who reaches the top?

HOPE SUCKS

I was at a Tony Robbins seminar last year when he said, "You know what? Hope sucks." I looked at my dad and started laughing. Hope sucks? Okay, I'm open-minded. Here is what he meant when he said this: You can hope all day long, or you can go out and do something to make your situation better.

These are some of my favorite Jim Rohn quotes; he had an amazing way of putting things in perspective:

Don't wish it were easier; wish you were better.
Don't wish for less problems; wish for more skills.

If you are reading this, you want to be better than good. You want to be better than great. You want to be exceptional. At last year's seminar Tony said if you are good, you'll get poor results; if you are great, you'll get good results; if you are outstanding, you'll get great results; but if you are exceptional, you'll get outstanding results. The difference between being great, outstanding, and exceptional is minor. Small changes in how you think, what you do, and how you act make all the difference in the world.

The slight edge, the little things, make the big difference. The difference between a struggling SendOutCards Manager and a successful Executive? Not much—just a few simple things. Read *The Slight Edge: Secret to a Successful Life* by Jeff Olson, and you will see that anyone can achieve extraordinary results when they have an edge working for them instead of against them.

With the right skills, the right attitude, commitment, and persistence, you can make your goals happen. You can have everything you ever dreamed of, but it takes commitment to getting better and better. Hope sucks!

CHAPTER 18

You Can't Control Duplication

Your goal in network marketing is to have a lot of people

doing a little, not a few people doing a lot.

DEMARR ZIMMERMAN

People ask me what I do to get duplication. I think no matter how many reps you have on your team, you want to have more, and you want it to grow faster. If you ask Jordan if he'd rather have 200 or 100 reps coming in every day, I know what his answer would be. Duplication is not something that can be forced. No matter what you do, your group will never duplicate as fast as you want it to. But here are some things I have learned to help support the duplication of your team.

YOUR TEAM WILL DO WHAT YOU DO, NOT WHAT YOU SAY

What are you doing in your own personal business? Are you bringing in reps? Are you doing the activities you are teaching?

YOUR NEW DISTRIBUTORS ARE NOT NEW
DISTRIBUTORS UNTIL THEY HAVE A NEW
DISTRIBUTOR

Focus on first becoming a Success Unit yourself, then helping your new people become Success Units. This business is built one brick and one Success Unit at a time. As you teach this over and over, the simplicity and consistency of the message will resonate through your team.

WORK WITH THOSE WHO DESERVE IT,
NOT THOSE WHO NEED IT

Guess what? Not every rep you sign up will work this as a business. Your goal is to help people get started, get their foundation set up, and help them start moving forward. Once you do that, you will find out very quickly who is serious and who is not. Your job is to find those serious people and act as their leader. You can't lead those that don't want to be led. Focus on those who deserve it, not those who need it.

LOCATE AND WORK YOUR "HOT POCKETS"

As your team grows, you will find groups sprouting out of nowhere. You will find someone on your fourth, fifth, or sixth level who is really working. This is called a hot pocket—someone who catches fire and goes to work. Reach out to them, lead them, and support them. Always be looking for these hot pockets because they will feed the depth of your organization, and depth provides secure residual income down the road.

NO MATTER WHAT HAPPENS, STAND TALL AND BE STRONG

As the leader, your group will look to you for direction. When you and your team are going through challenges or the company is growing through a transition, you have to be the one who carries them through. If you do a good job at this, your team will grow. If you don't, your team will stop. Be the one who carries the vision of Kody Bateman. Never let anything deter you from where you are going, and you will attract people to your business.

KEEP THE MESSAGE SIMPLE, CLEAR, AND CONSISTENT

Jordan Adler has kept his message simple, clear, and consistent since he joined SendOutCards. What message are you sending your team? Is it always changing? Keep things simple, and duplication will happen faster.

CHAPTER 19

Find Your Aces

Aces in your business will inspire you every day. When

you find an ace, everything changes.

Imagine you have a deck of cards. Every time you sponsor a new distributor into your business, you turn over one of the cards. When you turn over an ace, you have hit a home run. Aces are leaders. Aces are coachable. Aces show up, they do the work, and they get results. Aces are self-starters.

But first, are you an ace? I do believe leaders can be born that way, but I also believe people become leaders by working on themselves. And I believe you are an ace or you would not be reading this.

You already know this business will provide challenges and frustration, but I promise it is worth it. I heard an analogy from Everett O'Keefe at the Senior Manager event in San Jose—and whoever came up with it is genius!

Imagine you are sitting down with four of your new distributors. Each of them is holding a deck of cards. See if you recognize yourself in any of these four people and then choose which one works for you.

1) The first person holds the deck of cards out in front of them and just stares at them
This is the equivalent of doing nothing. You manage your team, you do a little, but you are not out there sponsoring new reps. Either you have sponsored a bunch and stopped, or you sponsored a few and they haven't done much, so you got tired of turning over cards. This is a dangerous place to be because you start blaming. Don't be the person staring at the deck of cards!

2) The second person turns over cards in the deck, but when he finds a 2, he takes a magic marker and crosses out the 2, then writes "ace" on it.
You find someone who has great potential, someone you think could be an ace. This person could be a superstar! You spend all your time with that new rep trying to get him or her to be an ace, rather than going out and sponsoring another distributor.

3) The third person turns cards over, but when he finds an ace, he has to take out a sheet of paper and write the numbers one to 100—only after he has done this is another card turned over.

You did it! You found an ace. However, you stop working. You spend *all* your time with that ace, helping move this person along, talking to your upline, or taking a vacation—everything *but* going out and finding another ace. Get back to work!

4) The fourth person keeps turning cards over on a regular basis, always looking for the ace, But even after finding one, she keeps flipping over cards.

You turn a card over and discover it's not an ace. So you turn over another card. Not an ace. You keep turning over cards. You don't stop. You know an ace is coming.

I instantly connected with this analogy because I have played all four of these roles at different points in my business. What hit home for me was knowing that when you flip over a card and don't have an ace, chances are better that the next card will be an ace. Sometimes you get an ace on the first card, or you might go through 48 cards and find the last four cards are aces.

Knowing that you have four aces in a deck, does it bother you that you might not find one right away? Do you keep flipping cards over, or do you stop because you are frustrated? My brother found an ace on the first card. I found one on about the fortieth card. I didn't know this analogy, but I *knew* I had aces coming.

I take the analogy one step further. I *know* I have four aces in every deck of cards. For every 52 people I sponsor, I *know* four will be aces. How many of us have that belief? You might not believe you have any aces in your deck—it is all in your mind. But if you *know* that for every card you turn over, the next one could be an ace, and the probability is just getting better and better, you will continue turning over cards. I *know* my deck of cards has aces in it; I just need to flip over more cards. I know I can't make someone an ace. And I know I can't just stare at the deck of cards. Every day in your business, you too are holding a deck of cards. The beautiful thing is *you* get to decide which type of person you are.

How should this change your business? Recognize every new person you sponsor gives you a chance to find an ace. But if you stop, you never get that chance. Stay the course, find the aces, but *believe* they are in your deck—and they will be.

CHAPTER 20

Freedom in Every Way is Possible

Ninety percent of my income comes from five key legs.

JORDAN ADLER

We are on an amazing journey. The great thing is we are on it together, and we can all learn from each other. I definitely don't have all the answers, but I'm smart enough to surround myself with the right people.

When I first started, I was looking for my first team builder. I was looking for the first person who would go out and do *something*. Once I found this person, my next goal was to find the person who would make Manager. Then someone to make Senior Manager. And someone to make Executive. It's amazing the journey of personal growth that happens in a business like SendOutCards.

You can achieve absolutely everything you can imagine. First, see it in your mind, then write it down, and take the steps to make it happen. Things don't necessarily happen overnight—they can, but if they don't, it is just part of the journey you are on. You already know you can't compare your business to someone else's.

I love talking about the dream network marketing provides because I am living my dream. However, I am just getting started. In the quote above, Jordan mentions that 90 percent of his income comes from five key legs. A key leg is group or team in your business that, if you were to go away, would continue to grow. Key legs are your key to freedom. Here is a fun thing to share with your team:

One key leg = a car payment
Two key legs = car and house payment
Three key legs = never work again
Four key legs = your previous yearly income becomes your monthy income
Five key legs = Your biggest challenges are how to reduce your taxable income, whether you want to go to Hawaii or Jamaica, and whether you should take the G5 or the Lear jet.

Can you see how it gets more and more exciting? Always be looking for and developing new distributors, and the longer you are in this business, the more key legs you will develop. I am excited every day because I have a couple key legs, but I know so much more is possible. Get back to dreaming because in this business, all of this and more is possible.

BE THE LEADER YOU WERE DESTINED TO BE

My goal when making this message into a presentation was to share the lessons I've learned in my business. I want to help everyone be successful and speed up the process and to prevent you from making some of the mistakes I've made. I have learned these things from other distributors, from my upline, and from Kody Bateman. I didn't come up with them; they are just lessons that stuck with me.

It is my goal for you to turn back to this when you get stuck, to share it with your team so they know what it takes to build the business, and to be the leader you were destined to be. We all have greatness inside; sometimes it just takes a little push or the right business to bring it out.

I look forward to hearing of your success and watching you stroll across stage to receive your promotion and hug from Kody B. We all deserve to be, do, and have everything we want in this life. Now is your time. Go out and make it happen.